Famous Places of the World

North America

Helen Bateman and Jayne Denshire

Smart Apple Media

Smart Apple Media
2140 Howard Drive West
North Mankato
Minnesota 56003

First published in 2006 by
MACMILLAN EDUCATION AUSTRALIA PTY LTD
627 Chapel Street, South Yarra, Australia 3141

Visit our Web site at www.macmillan.com.au

Associated companies and representatives throughout the world.

Copyright © Helen Bateman and Jayne Denshire 2006

Library of Congress Cataloging-in-Publication Data

Bateman, Helen.
    North America / by Helen Bateman and Jayne Denshire.
      p. cm. — (Famous places of the world)
    Includes bibliographical references and index.
    ISBN-13: 978-1-58340-802-5 (alk. paper)
    1. North America—History, Local—Juvenile literature. 2. Historic sites—North America—Juvenile
    literature. 3. North America—Description and travel—Juvenile literature. I. Denshire, Jayne.
    II. Title. III. Series: Bateman, Helen. Famous places of the world.

    E38.5.B37 2006
    970—dc22   2006002574

Project management by Limelight Press Pty Ltd
Design by Stan Lamond, Lamond Art & Design
Illustrations by Marjorie Crosby-Fairall
Maps by Lamond Art & Design and Andrew Davies
Map icons by Andrew Davies
Research by Kathy Gerrard
Consultant: Colin Sale BA (Sydney) MSc (London)

Printed in USA

Acknowledgments
The authors and the publisher are grateful to the following for permission to reproduce
copyright material:

Cover photograph: Grand Canyon, courtesy of APL/Corbis/Danny Lehman
APL/Corbis/Roger Ressmeyer p. 11 (top); APL/Corbis/Richard Glover p. 11 (bottom); APL/Corbis/
Angelo Hornak p. 14; APL/Corbis p. 18, APL/Corbis/Joseph Sohm p. 19, APL/Corbis p. 21; Getty
Images/Andy Caulfield p. 7; Getty Images/Altrendo Travel p. 23 (top); iStockphoto/Rob MacDonald
p. 4 (left); iStockphoto/Michael Puerzer p. 4 (right); iStockphoto/Ralf Stadtaus p. 6; iStockphoto/
Amy Seagram p. 9 (bottom); iStockphoto/Steve Geer p. 16; iStockphoto/Tom Garvin p. 17 (top left);
iStockphoto/Angelika Stern p. 22; iStockphoto/Ben Renard-Wiart p. 25 (bottom); iStockphoto/
Nicholas Belton p. 28; Lonely Planet/Neil Setchfield p. 9 (top); Lonely Planet/Richard l'Anson
p. 15; Lonely Planet/Kim Grant p. 23 (bottom); Lonely Planet/Kraig Lieb p. 24; Lonely Planet/Alfredo
Maiquez p. 26; Lonely Planet/Andrew Marshall and Leonie Walker p. 27; Lonely Planet/Richard
Cummins p. 29; Michael Pawlyk/Photolibrary.com p. 8; Kenneth M. Highfill/Photolibrary.com p. 12;
Amy and Chuck Wiley/photolibrary.com p. 13; Worldsat Int. inc/SPL/photolibrary.com p. 20.

While every care has been taken to trace and acknowledge copyright, the publisher tenders their
apologies for any accidental infringement where copyright has proved untraceable. Where the attempt
has been unsuccessful, the publisher welcomes information that would redress the situation.

Contents

When a word in the text is printed in **bold**. You can look up its meaning in the Glossary on page 31.

Wonders of North America

North America is a **continent** with almost every type of wonder. Rugged mountains, unique national parks, desert areas, and some of the largest cities in the world are all part of the varied landscape. There are many famous places in North America. Some are ancient and some are modern. Some are natural wonders and some have been built by humans.

What makes a place famous?

The most common reasons why places become famous are because of their:

- **formation** how they were formed by nature
- **construction** how they were built by humans
- **antiquity** their age, dating back to ancient times
- **size** their height, width, length, volume, or area
- **function** how they work, or what they are used for
- **cultural importance** their value to the customs and society of the country
- **religious importance** their value to the religious beliefs of the country

ZOOM IN
The oldest built structures in North America are in Mexico.

Famous places in North America

North America has many famous places. Some are built structures and some are features created by nature.

Statue of Liberty

The Statue of Liberty is a built structure that is famous for its size and cultural importance. It stands on Liberty Island in New York Harbour and is the city's most famous landmark.

A womanly statue

This huge copper-covered statue shows a woman dressed in Roman clothes holding a torch in her right hand. In her other hand is a piece of stone with the date of America's independence carved on it. The seven rays on her crown symbolize freedom, or liberty, spreading to the seven continents and seas of the world. She is standing on chains as a sign of the end of slavery. Once slavery ended, slaves never had to wear chains again.

ZOOM IN
The statue arrived from France 10 years late because of building and cost difficulties.

◄ One fingernail on the statue's hand is the size of a large book, and the nose is 4.9 feet (1.5 m) long, illustrating the enormous scale of this structure.

iron skeleton

spiral staircase

► The statue is hollow inside and has an iron skeleton. A double spiral staircase runs up through the center of the statue's body.

▲ The harbour location of the Statue of Liberty means it is the first thing people see when they arrive in New York by boat.

A gift from France

The Statue of Liberty was given as a gift of friendship to the United States from France. The French people were in charge of building the statue itself. The completed statue weighed 224 tons (228 t) so it was far too heavy to move in one piece. It was separated into 350 bits, packed into over 200 cases then sent to the United States by sea. It was put together after it arrived and was unveiled in 1886.

Today, this mighty landmark is known throughout the world.

INSIDE STORY

The day the Statue of Liberty was unveiled was the day the 'ticker-tape parade' was born. Over 1 million people filled the streets of New York City while office workers above them threw rolls of tape, or ticker, out the windows to mark the occasion.

ZOOM IN

Winds of up to 50 miles (80 km) per hour cause the statue to sway 3 inches (7.5 cm) and the torch to sway 5 inches (13 cm).

Niagara Falls

ZOOM IN

Almost 20 percent of the world's fresh water flows over Niagara Falls.

FACT FINDER

Location border of United States and Canada

Date formed 10,000 years ago

Height 164 feet (50 m)

Length more than 3,280 feet (1,000 m)

▼ Horseshoe Falls and American Falls make up Niagara Falls. They are separated by the tree-covered Goat Island.

Niagara Falls is a natural landform that is famous for its formation, size, and beauty. It is made up of two separate falls, American Falls and Horseshoe Falls, with an island between them. At the end of the Niagara River, water plunges over cliffs at these two places into a deep **gorge** below.

Two falls become one

Horseshoe Falls is the larger of the two falls that make up Niagara Falls and lies in Canada. It drops more water over a greater distance. American Falls is smaller than Horseshoe Falls because it drops less water, and is straighter in shape. It lies in the United States. The tremendous volume of water that falls over the cliffs never stops flowing. So much water falls that the sound it makes is deafening.

Goat Island

Horseshoe Falls

American Falls

◄ A boat called the Maid of the Mist takes people into the churning waters of the gorge below Horseshoe Falls. A fine mist from the falls always fills the air.

ZOOM IN

Two cities, both named Niagara Falls, are beside the falls. One city is in Canada and the other is in the United States.

Turning ice to water

Niagara Falls was formed just over 10,000 years ago at the end of the last **ice age**. Back then, the point that the water falls over was 17 miles (11 km) further forward. Over thousands of years, the rocky cliffs have been **eroded** by the water constantly crashing over them and a deep gorge has been formed.

Niagara Falls is one of the most famous natural wonders in the world because of the huge volume of water that falls over its cliffs.

► Horseshoe Falls gets its name from its shape. More than 440,000 gallons (2 million l) of water fall over the cliffs per second at 68 miles (110 km) per hour.

Golden Gate Bridge

The Golden Gate Bridge is a built structure that is famous for its construction. It is one of the largest and most spectacular suspension bridges in the world. It stretches across the entrance of San Francisco Bay, linking the city of San Francisco to northern California. Earthquakes hit this area quite often, so the bridge has been built to withstand their effects.

A supported roadway

Like all suspension bridges, this bridge has a roadway that hangs from steel cables that are supported by two towers. The roadway has six lanes and is 220 feet (67 m) above the water. The bridge design is in the **Art Deco** style of architecture with its elegant curved shapes and its rectangular upright supports.

During construction, a safety net was set up beneath the bridge, which saved the lives of around 19 workers.

ZOOM IN
The toll charged for using the bridge is ten times more today than it was when the bridge opened in 1937.

◄ The bridge is fitted with special warning lights that help guide sea and air travelers at night.

ZOOM IN
A fog horn sounds on the bridge for 2.5 hours per day on average, and up to 5 hours in the foggy season.

In all kinds of weather

All sorts of problems had to be thought about when the bridge was being built, such as bad weather and the chance of earthquakes. In December, there are often dangerous winds with gusts of over 62 miles (100 km) per hour. These can mean that the bridge needs to be closed. During the foggy season from July to October, fog horns sound to guide ships safely under the bridge.

Despite these challenges, the Golden Gate Bridge remains one of the most famous bridges in the world.

▲ The bridge has always been painted red so it can be easily seen in heavy fog. It is painted regularly to protect its steel surface from rusting in the salt air.

▼ Suspension bridges such as the Golden Gate Bridge are often used to link two places that are separated by a great distance.

Grand Canyon

The Grand Canyon is a natural landform that is famous for its size and formation. It stretches as far as the eye can see with many horizontal layers of different colored rocks. This massive canyon has been carved to this great depth by the fast-flowing waters of the Colorado River. Other **canyons** run into the Grand Canyon, and together they form the Grand Canyon National Park.

▼ The spectacular colors in the walls of the Grand Canyon come from the different types and ages of rock.

An ancient formation

The Grand Canyon has been forming for the past 10 million years. The land was raised above sea level about 10 million years ago. At that time, the Colorado River began carving its channel deep into the many layers of rock beneath it. The river flowed so rapidly with so much water over a long time that it cut through these rock layers right down to the oldest rocks of all at the bottom.

Rock walls

The different types of rock in the walls of the canyon give it its distinctive shape and color. The softer limestones, which are lighter in color, erode more quickly than harder rocks and produce more gentle slopes in the canyon walls. Harder rocks, such as shale and sandstone, are eroded into steeper slopes. The oldest rocks are at the bottom of the canyon and are granite, over 2 billion years old.

The formation of the Grand Canyon make it one of the world's great natural wonders.

▲ One of the most thrilling ways to experience the Grand Canyon is to raft down the Colorado River. This is the wildest stretch of white water in the United States.

City of Teotihuacán

The ancient city of Teotihuacán is a built landmark that is famous for its antiquity and construction. It is not clear who built the city originally. It was built and then destroyed hundreds of years before the local Indian people, the Aztecs, discovered its ruins and settled there. The Aztecs lived in Central Mexico in the 1500s.

Archeologists believe that Teotihuacán was a busy trading center and one of the largest cities in the world at the time it was built. The city had about 2,000 single-story buildings and great temples, squares, and palaces for priests and kings. Merchants sold their goods in the central squares and farmers worked the local fields.

▼ The city was laid out in a grid pattern with the buildings placed in rows at right angles to each other. This view shows the central zone and is taken from the Pyramid of the Moon.

Pyramid of the Sun

Cuidadela (Temple of Quetzalcoatl)

Avenue of the Dead

Pyramid of the Moon

Ancient high-rise

Two pyramids rise above the house sites and temples. They are the Pyramid of the Sun and the Pyramid of the Moon. The Pyramid of the Sun was one of the largest structures ever built in the ancient Americas. In the 1970s, an internal tunnel was discovered in the pyramid that led to a set of secret chambers, or rooms. The Pyramid of the Moon is at the other end of the site. It has a series of smaller pyramids inside it and a **tomb** that contains the remains of a male skeleton and gifts to the gods.

City center

The main street of Teotihuacán was called the Avenue of the Dead and ran down the center of the city past the main square, called the Cuidadela. It was 1.5 miles (2.5 km) long. The Temple of Quetzalcoatl was at the Cuidadela. Burial sites have been found around this temple containing many skeletons.

This ancient ruin is now one of the most famous archeological discoveries in the world.

ZOOM IN
The god Quetzalcoatl was named because he had quetzal bird feathers instead of scales.

▲ The walls of the Temple of Quetzalcoatl are decorated with many stone heads of Quetzalcoatl, the feathered serpent god.

ZOOM IN
The city was trashed and burned in 750 A.D. and then turned to ruin. Hundreds of years later, the area became an Aztec settlement.

INSIDE STORY

Aztec priests performed strange rituals in the temples on top of the pyramids to keep the sun on its daily path. They cut the beating heart out of their human victims and let the blood flow down the steps. A number of the ancient American civilizations were known for these rituals.

Rocky Mountains

The Rocky Mountains are a natural landform that are famous for their size and beauty. They run down the western side of the North American continent, from Alaska in the north to Mexico in the south.

The Rocky Mountains are divided into four regions. The Arctic Rockies are in the far north, the Northern, or Canadian, Rockies run through Canada into the United States, the Middle Rockies run through the southern United States, and the Southen Rockies run down to New Mexico.

Beautiful creations

The Rockies were created millions of years ago as a result of some severe upheaval in the Earth's **crust**. Since then, very big **glaciers** and rivers have worn away the rocky landscape to create the breathtaking scenery seen today.

▼ Some of the world's most beautiful scenery is in the Canadian Rockies, such as thick forests, crystal-clear lakes and snowy peaks.

▲ The dazzling mountain scenery and tree-lined walking tracks make hiking a popular outdoor activity.

Seasonal changes

The seasons vary from one part of the Rockies to another. Summers are usually mild and winters are cold, however the climate changes rapidly as the **altitude** increases.

Many creatures, such as moose, deer, and pumas have adapted to the mountainous environment by developing **sure-footedness**. Some animals, such as black bears, **hibernate** to escape the harsh winters and have developed big feet so they can walk in the snow. Others, such as caribou, **migrate** to lower, warmer areas.

High mountains, deep valleys, rivers, national parks, and wildlife all combine to make the Rocky Mountains one of the world's most beautiful natural wonders.

▲ The Arctic Rockies in the far north are permanently snow-covered. They join the Northern Rockies in Canada.

ZOOM IN
In winter, some animals shed their brown coat and replace it with white fur so they blend in with the snow.

Empire State Building

ZOOM IN

The Empire State Building is struck by lightning about 100 times a year.

FACT FINDER

Location New York City, United States

Date built 1930–1932

Height 1,453 feet (443 m)

The Empire State Building is a built structure that is famous for its size and construction. It stands in the center of New York City and provides the city's most spectacular view with an open-air viewing terrace on the 86th floor. It was the world's tallest building until 1972, when the former World Trade Center was built. Now, Taipei 101 in Taiwan is the world's tallest building and the Empire State Building is the ninth tallest.

A multi-storey marvel

The Art Deco building has 102 stories which reach a height of 1,250 feet (381 m). In 1950 a broadcasting tower was added, increasing the height to 1,473 feet (449 m). However the building "shrank" in 1985 when a new, shorter antenna was erected, which brought it back to 1,453 feet (443 m). The building was built in record time and on budget. This was an unusual result for a building of its size.

ZOOM IN

The Empire State Building is so tall that when people on the 86th floor are standing in sunshine, it can be raining on the streets below.

◄ In the 1930s, the needle-like spire on top of the building was trialed as a depot for zeppelin aircraft. However the idea proved unsuccessful so it was discontinued.

► The outside of the building is made up of 10 million bricks and 215,280 square feet (20,000 sq m) of windows.

A Raskob design

John Jacob Raskob was the designer of the building. He wanted a skyscraper that would be bigger and better than the Chrysler building, built in New York around the same time. Raskob designed his building to look like a pencil and soar higher into the air than any structure on Earth. Once the building was finished, he reached his goal.

Today, this world-famous structure attracts thousands of people each year who marvel at its structure.

INSIDE STORY

When the Empire State Building was finished in 1932, the United States was in the middle of the Depression, a time when people had little money to spend on rent. Space in he building was hard for developers to let, which led to the building being nicknamed "Empty State Building."

viewing terrace

Great Lakes

The Great Lakes are natural features that are famous for their size and formation. The five lakes of Erie, Ontario, Huron, Michigan, and Superior make up the largest body of fresh water in the world.

Formed from ice

The lakes were formed during the ice ages of Earth's history over 10,000 years ago. The snow that fell over Canada, which was a very cold environment then, did not melt, and formed a huge ice sheet which moved slowly south. This huge glacier eroded the surface it moved over and cut more deeply into areas with softer rocks. When the ice finally melted, the deepest areas filled with water to form the lakes.

From the 1600s, the waterways provided an easy transportation route for European explorers and settlers, in search of new land in Canada.

FACT FINDER

Location border of United States and Canada

Date formed 11,000–15,000 years ago

Size 94,595 square miles (245,000 sq km)

ZOOM IN

The area covered by the Great Lakes is the same size as the United Kingdom.

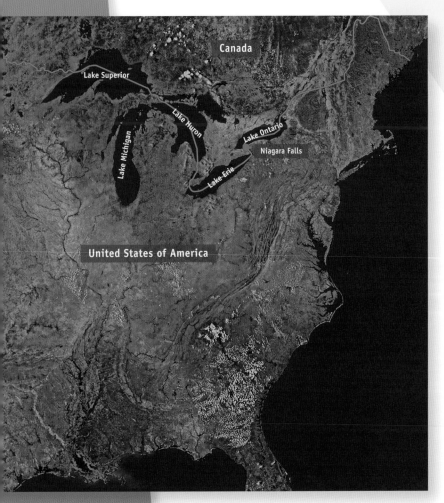

Canada

Lake Superior

Lake Huron

Lake Michigan

Lake Ontario

Niagara Falls

Lake Erie

United States of America

◄ Lake Superior is the largest and deepest lake. Lake Erie is the shallowest lake and flows over Niagara Falls into Lake Ontario.

Work and play

The Great Lakes are a great natural resource. They supply cities with fresh water, generate **hydroelectricity** for industries such as car production, and provide easy transportation from the interior of North America to the coast.

Birds are common on the lakes' shores, and the nearby small islands are nesting grounds for ring-billed gulls and terns.

Outdoor recreation is popular on the various beaches in summer. The formation of, and activity around, the Great Lakes contribute to their worldwide fame.

ZOOM IN

When the "White Hurricane" storm of 1913 hit the Great Lakes, it caused winds of 90 miles (145 km) per hour, waves over 36 feet (11 m) high and thick snow storms.

▼ The city of Chicago lies on Lake Michigan in the United States. Parts of the four other lakes are in Canada.

Pyramid of the Magician

ZOOM IN
Pyramid of the Magician gets its name from a popular myth. The myth says a dwarf with magical powers built the pyramid in one night.

FACT FINDER

Location Uxmal ruins, Yucatan Peninsula, Mexico

Date built 800s A.D.

Height 131 feet (40 m)

Size of base 226 feet (69 m) long and 161 feet (49 m) wide

WORLD HERITAGE SITE since 1996

The Pyramid of the Magician is a built structure that is famous for its cultural and religious importance, and its construction. It is the tallest structure in the ancient ruins of Uxmal, the greatest **Mayan** city from the 600s A.D. to the 900s A.D. The pyramid was built from limestone in stages, then re-built over a period of about 300 years.

A religious center

Uxmal was a center for religious ceremonies. Only rulers, priests, and officials lived in the center. Mayan peasants lived in communities in the nearby jungle.

The pyramid was built in the Puuc architectural style. This style used limestone construction and rough plaster finishes. The pyramid's design had strong horizontal lines and featured masks of the rain god, Chac, on the stone work.

ZOOM IN
Mayan stonemasons fitted stones so tightly together that a knife blade could not slide between them, even today.

◄ Like all Mayan pyramids, the Pyramid of the Magician had a temple sitting on top. This is because it was thought to be at the closest point to the heavens.

Pyramid of the Magician

▲ The Pyramid of the Magician stands in the center of the ancient ruins at Uxmal.

Temples, not tombs

Temples, rather than tombs, were built in Mayan pyramids. The temples were quite small inside, with two or three cramped rooms used for religious ceremonies. The rooms contained altars and stone platforms where the priests made their offerings to the gods. Animals, including deer and turkey, were often put forward as altar gifts to feed the gods and make them happy.

The construction of this pyramid and its role in Mayan culture make it one of the most famous ancient structures in the world.

► A steep staircase leads up to the entrance of the temple that sits on top of the pyramid.

Yellowstone National Park

FACT FINDER

Location **Wyoming, United States**

Date formed **60,000 years ago**

Size **3,470 square miles
(8,980 sq km)**

WORLD HERITAGE SITE
  since 1978

Yellowstone National Park is a natural feature that is famous for its beauty and formation. It is the oldest national park in the world and has important **geothermal** features, such as hot springs and **geysers**. The landscape consists of a number of broad **plateaus** enclosed by **ridges** and **peaks** with a multitude of wildlife in the mountains and valleys.

▼ Most of Yellowstone National Park is covered in pine forests. A number of rivers flow through the region, too.

ZOOM IN
Wolves were re-introduced to the park as hunters for the larger, sick animals. Before this, the animals were left to slowly die because they had no natural predator.

▲ Bison are among the wide variety of wildlife that lives in Yellowstone National Park.

Geysers and hot springs

Yellowstone has more than 200 active geysers and 10,000 hot springs that are the result of previous volcanic eruptions. Beneath the surface of Yellowstone National Park is a mass of molten rock, called magma. This keeps the rocks on top hot. These rocks heat the waters which seep into the ground to produce the many hot springs. Some of these springs become super hot, turn to steam and explode into the air as geysers. The time between geyser eruptions can vary from minutes to a number of months.

ZOOM IN
Old Faithful, the most famous geyser in the park, erupts every 73 minutes on average and spouts a gush of hot water and steam 115 feet (35 m) into the air.

Wildlife

Mountain goats, deer, and elk roam the rugged mountain areas of Yellowstone, and fish swim in the rivers and lakes. The rare trumpeter swan is one of the many species of bird life found in the park.

Natural beauty and unique formations combine to create this world-famous natural wonder.

► Hot springs are a common sight in Yellowstone. Algae and bacteria thrive in the warm waters and give the springs their vivid color.

Panama Canal

The Panama Canal is a built structure that is famous for its construction and function. This artificial waterway cuts through a narrow strip of land, called an isthmus, between North and South America. The canal allows ships to travel directly from one side of America to the other without having to take the long and dangerous trip around Cape Horn at the southern tip of South America.

The canal has six **locks**, which allow ships to be raised or lowered over higher land by creating steps with different water levels.

► More than 30 ships use the Panama Canal each day and take around 8 hours to go from one end to the other.

INSIDE STORY

The idea for the Panama Canal began back in the 1500s when some European countries wanted a quicker route to the "New World" where riches were to be found. It was not until 1882 that a French company tried to build the canal. They set about preparing the land, but the task proved too hard and the project was canceled.

ZOOM IN

To travel from San Francisco to New York by sea via the Panama Canal is 5,200 miles (8,370 km) compared to 12,990 miles (20,900 km) via South America. This is a short cut of 7,790 miles (12,530 km).

An ambitious project

The Panama Canal was thought to be the most ambitious engineering feat of its time. An artificial lake was formed by damming a river and excavating massive areas of rock at the highest part of the isthmus. Huge areas of jungle and swamp were cleared using steam shovels and **dredges**. Then locks were built to raise and lower ships in steps of water up to the lake level and down the other side.

The greatest challenge

The greatest challenge during the construction of the Panama Canal was excavating the solid rock at a point called the Galliard Cut. Massive layers of rock had to be cut away to create a valley. The movement of the hard rock often caused landslides. This world-famous waterway has greatly improved ship travel in the United States.

▲ The lock gates open when the water level is the same on both sides of the gates.

ZOOM IN

The amount of earth removed during construction of the canal was thought to fill the same space as several city buildings 19 miles (30 km) high.

▼ The locks are like lifts. They raise ships from sea level up to the level of the lake then back down to sea level once they pass through the lake.

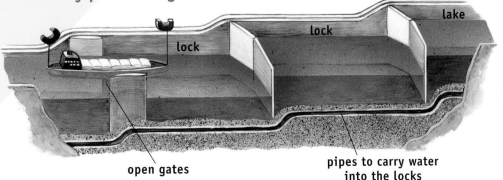

lake

lock

lock

open gates

pipes to carry water into the locks

White House

FACT FINDER

Location Washington DC, United States

Date built 1792–1800

Area covered 9 hectares (22 ac)

National Historic Landmark since 1960

The White House is a built structure that is famous for its construction and function. It is the oldest government building in Washington DC, the nation's capital, and the home and workplace for the President of the United States.

▼ The official address of the White House is 1,600 Pennsylvania Avenue, Washington DC. Virtually every US President has lived there since 1800.

► The President's office, known as the Oval Office, is in the West Wing. Many famous meetings with world leaders are held here.

More stories below than above

The White House is six stories high, but much of the building is below ground level so it looks smaller than it really is. Two wings, known as the East Wing and the West Wing, are located on either side of the main building. In the East Wing is an underground space built during World War II for emergency operations. The area is still used today.

A president's home

The President's family lives in the main building. A range of facilities is offered for the President, his family, and guests including a tennis court, swimming pool, jogging track, and bowling lane.

Five chefs are employed to provide meals for up to 140 guests at a time. The kitchen staff can prepare more than 1,000 food items in one session. As the presidential home and workplace, the White House is one of America's most famous built structures.

Famous places of North America

Our world has a rich collection of famous places. Some are spectacular natural wonders and some are engineering or architectural masterpieces. These famous places in North America are outstanding in many different ways.

Wonders formed by nature

PLACE	FAMOUS FOR
Niagara Falls	The second largest body of falling water in the world
Grand Canyon	Some of the oldest rocks in the world and some of the deepest gorges
Rocky Mountains	The largest mountain system in North America Spectacular scenery and outdoor activities
Great Lakes	The largest group of freshwater lakes in the world The most important inland waterway in North America
Yellowstone National Park	The oldest national park in the world Geysers and hot springs, and spectacular natural scenery

Masterpieces built by humans

PLACE	FAMOUS FOR
Statue of Liberty	Its enormous size and its symbolism
Golden Gate Bridge	One of the largest suspension bridges in the world
City of Teotihuacán	An ancient ruin and one of the largest cities in the world between 100 A.D. and 750 A.D.
Empire State Building	The tallest building in the world until 1972 Spectacular views as far as the eye can see
Pyramid of the Magician	Tallest structure in the Mayan ruin of Uxmal
Panama Canal	One of the greatest engineering feats of the 1900s Revolutionized world shipping patterns
White House	Home and workplace for the President of the United States

Glossary

altitude height above sea level

archeologists people who study the people and customs of ancient times from the buildings they left behind

Art Deco a style of decoration from the 1920s and 1930s that used geometric shapes

canyons deep valleys with steep sides

continent one of the main land masses of the world

crust the hard outer surface of Earth

dredges machines for drawing up sand or mud from the bottom of rivers and harbours

eroded broken down and worn away by the elements of the weather such as water, wind, and ice

geothermal caused by heat from the core of Earth

geysers hot springs that sometimes shoot jets of water and steam into the air

glaciers large areas of snow that become hard like ice and move slowly down a mountain

gorge a narrow alley with steep, rocky walls on both sides of a river or stream

hibernate to have a long deep sleep during winter, often underground

hydroelectricity electricity produced using falling water as a source of power

ice age a time in history when glacial ice covered much of Earth's surface

locks parts of a canal with gates at each end allowing ships to be raised or lowered from one level to another

Mayan belonging to the Maya, an indigenous group of people living in Yucatan, Mexico, between the 600s and 900s

migrate to move in a particular season from one habitat to another

peaks the tops of mountains

plateaus large flat stretches of high ground

ridges long narrow sections of high land

sure-footedness able to move without stumbling or falling, especially on rough or steep ground

tomb a grave, especially for important people

Index